I SPY

WITH MY LITTLE EYE

ANIMALS
VOLUME 1

LET'S PLAY I SPY

MEZZO
ZENTANGLE
DESIGNS

I SPY WITH MY LITTLE EYE SOMETHING BEGINNING WITH...

 **IS FOR**

ALLIGATOR

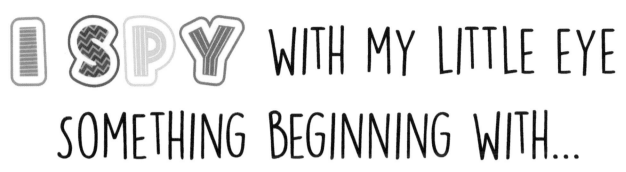

I SPY WITH MY LITTLE EYE SOMETHING BEGINNING WITH...

 IS FOR

I SPY WITH MY LITTLE EYE SOMETHING BEGINNING WITH...

 IS FOR

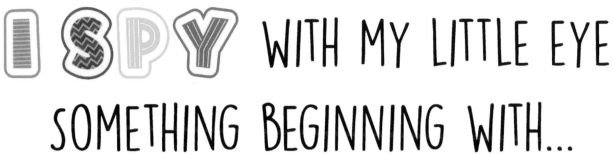

I SPY WITH MY LITTLE EYE SOMETHING BEGINNING WITH...

D IS FOR

DOG

I SPY WITH MY LITTLE EYE SOMETHING BEGINNING WITH...

 IS FOR

I SPY WITH MY LITTLE EYE SOMETHING BEGINNING WITH...

 IS FOR

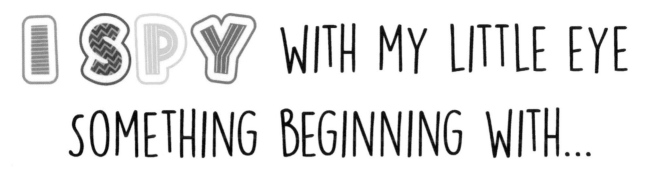

I SPY WITH MY LITTLE EYE SOMETHING BEGINNING WITH...

G IS FOR

GIRAFFE

I SPY WITH MY LITTLE EYE SOMETHING BEGINNING WITH...

H

H IS FOR

HAMSTER

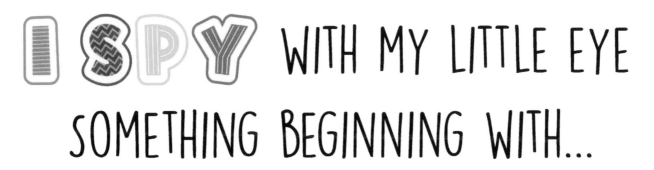

I SPY WITH MY LITTLE EYE SOMETHING BEGINNING WITH...

H IS FOR

HIPPO

 WITH MY LITTLE EYE SOMETHING BEGINNING WITH...

I IS FOR

IGUANA

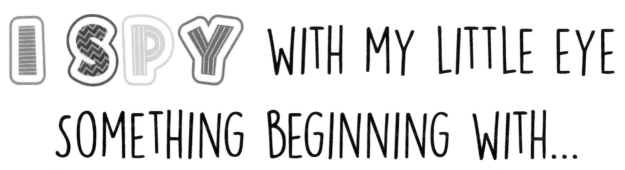

I SPY WITH MY LITTLE EYE SOMETHING BEGINNING WITH...

J IS FOR

JAGUAR

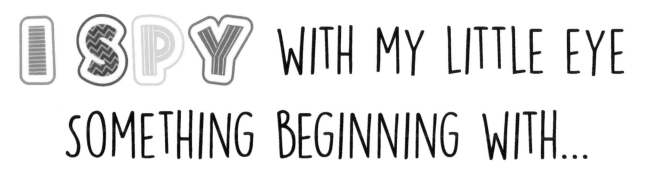

I SPY WITH MY LITTLE EYE SOMETHING BEGINNING WITH...

K IS FOR KOALA

I SPY WITH MY LITTLE EYE
SOMETHING BEGINNING WITH...

L IS FOR

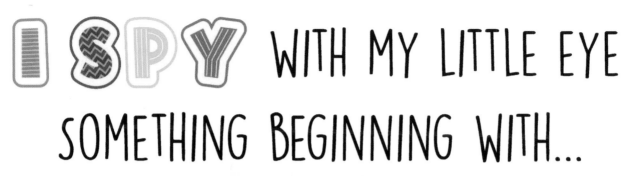

I SPY WITH MY LITTLE EYE SOMETHING BEGINNING WITH...

 IS FOR

 WITH MY LITTLE EYE SOMETHING BEGINNING WITH...

P IS FOR PANDA

I SPY WITH MY LITTLE EYE SOMETHING BEGINNING WITH...

 IS FOR

 WITH MY LITTLE EYE SOMETHING BEGINNING WITH...

IS FOR

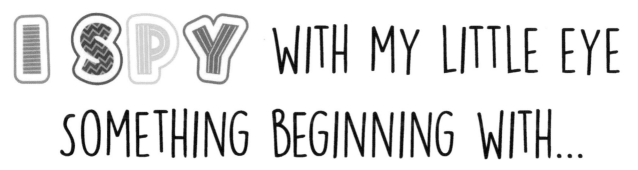

I SPY WITH MY LITTLE EYE SOMETHING BEGINNING WITH...

T IS FOR

TIGER

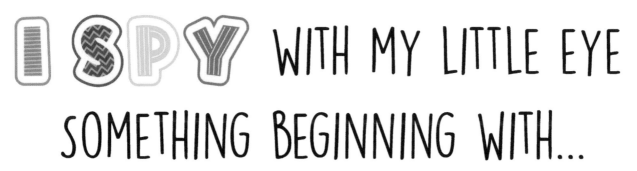

I SPY WITH MY LITTLE EYE SOMETHING BEGINNING WITH...

Y IS FOR

YAK

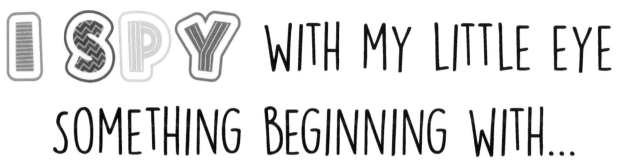

I SPY WITH MY LITTLE EYE SOMETHING BEGINNING WITH...

 IS FOR

Printed in Great Britain
by Amazon

15141578R00025